PRIVATE LABELLING

— A —

~~PAINFUL~~ GAINFUL JOURNEY

GET 3X GROWTH WITH
"MERI FACTORY WALA TRUST" EVERYTIME

PRIVATE LABELLING

— A —

~~PAINFUL~~ GAINFUL JOURNEY

GET 3X GROWTH WITH
"MERI FACTORY WALA TRUST" EVERYTIME

ADITYA DALMIA

ADITYA GOYAL

Worldwide Published by
Pendown Press

PENDOWN PRESS LLP
An ISO 9001 & ISO 14001 Certified Co.,
Regd. Office: 3767A, Kanhaiya Nagar,
Tri Nagar, Delhi-110035
Ph.: 8130886000, 9650072927
E-mail: info@pendownpress.com
Branch Office: 1A/2A, 20, Hari Sadan, Ansari Road,
Daryaganj, New Delhi-110002
Ph.: 011-45794768
Website: PendownPress.com

Edition: 2025
Price: ₹ 399
ISBN: 978-93-6338-420-0

Layout and Cover Designed by Pendown Graphics Team
Printed and Bound in India by Thomson Press India Ltd.

To the Dreamers and Doers
This book is dedicated to everyone with a vision
to create their own brand—whether you're a
startup, a brand owner, a large company, or
simply someone with a big dream.

Contents

Acknowledgements

My parents, are my greatest role models. Their unwavering love, guidance, and values have brought me to where I am today. I am truly grateful for everything they have done.

To my wife, who has stood by me in every situation. You have handled all family responsibilities with great skill and dedication. Thank you from the bottom of my heart.

To my children, who are the source of my happiness and inspiration. Sending you lots of love!

To my team at **Annakosha Pvt. Ltd.**, who have been like partners, mentors, and family. Thank you for walking this journey with me.

To our customers, who have shared their experiences and knowledge with us during this journey—thank you for trusting us and being our inspiration.

To my friend, Mr. Dinesh Verma, CEO of Pendown Press, and his team, who supported us throughout this creative process and provided great suggestions.

To the universe for giving me the ideas and strength to complete this book. I am grateful for the love, support, and guidance at every step.

And finally, to all my loved ones who have been with me on this journey—thank you for your unwavering support, encouragement, and affection. Even if your names are not mentioned, you always hold a special place in my heart.

Without the support of all of you, it would not have been possible for me to move forward with confidence.

Preface

Imagine this: You're sitting with your morning chai or coffee, thinking about your next big move. Maybe you're dreaming of launching your own food brand. Or perhaps you already have a business and are tired of the constant hustle to stay ahead. Sound familiar? Don't worry, you're not alone!

The food industry is not just about taste anymore; it's about staying ahead in a game that's changing faster than ever. From consumer demands for healthier snacks to the explosion of private labeling, the opportunities for growth are endless. But here's the catch: you need the right strategy to grab them. That's where Vishnu Delight comes into play—a name synonymous with success, innovation, and scaling smarter, not harder.

This isn't your typical "how-to" guide filled with boring jargon and vague theories. Nope. This book is designed to be your personal toolkit—practical, engaging, and downright transformative. Whether you're dreaming of launching your private label or scaling your existing brand to 3x growth, you'll find everything you need here.

We've packed in some real success stories, easy-to-follow frameworks, and even a few "aha!" moments to make your journey smoother. And don't worry—there's plenty of humor to keep things light because, let's face it, running a business is serious enough!

So, grab your favorite snack (you'll need it—this book might make you hungry), and dive in. Whether you want to turn your vision into a thriving brand or take your company to the next level, this book will guide you every step of the way.

Ready? Your success story starts here!

Whom This Book is For?

This book is for anyone and everyone who dreams big! Whether you're:

➤ A large company owner from the food industry or beyond, looking to expand your portfolio.

➤ A startup entrepreneur ready to make your mark with your very own brand.

➤ An individual with a vision, who believes the private labeling game (especially in food) is the next big thing and wants to ride the wave of its incredible growth.

We've designed this book to guide anyone who wants to explore private labeling, scale effortlessly, and build something that truly stands out. If you're wondering, "Can I be a Vishnu Delight client?" the answer is probably YES!

From seasoned business owners to first-time brand builders, this book is your roadmap to success. Whatever your background, if you've got the drive, we've got the tools to help you make it happen. Let's get started!

CHAPTER 1

Introduction to Private Labeling

What is Private Labeling?

Private labeling is a business strategy where products are sold under your brand instead of someone else's. Imagine you want to launch a food product, but you don't have the resources or expertise to manufacture it. That's where private labeling steps in. You choose a product, give it your brand name, design the packaging, and the manufacturer does all the work—right from production to quality checks.

This approach allows anyone to create their own brand—whether it's a brand owner in the food industry, a startup entrepreneur, or an individual passionate about launching something new. Private labeling gives you the power to bring your vision to life without the hassle of building everything from scratch.

Why Private Labels Matter in FMCG

In today's fast-moving consumer goods (FMCG) market, competition is fierce. Every day, new products, flavors, and innovations are launched. Consumers are always looking for something fresh, and businesses must stay ahead of these trends.

Investing in research, development, and manufacturing for every idea can be expensive and risky. Private labeling provides a cost-effective solution. Instead of investing heavily in infrastructure or manpower, businesses can collaborate with manufacturers who specialize in their desired product. This saves time and money while allowing companies to test the market with minimal risk.

Why is this approach so popular?

➢ **Cost-Effective:** No need for expensive equipment or R&D investments.

➢ **Faster Market Entry:** Products can be launched quickly.

➢ **Expertise Utilization:** Leverage the manufacturer's experience and resources.

➢ **Lower Risk:** If the product doesn't perform well, losses are minimal.

Private labeling lets businesses focus on branding and marketing while leaving production to the experts.

Overview of the Market and Emerging Trends

Private labeling is growing rapidly, especially in FMCG. Consumers are shifting their preferences toward brands they trust, whether it's a local entrepreneur or a retailer offering private-label products.

Here's why private labeling is thriving:

➢ **Local Trust:** Indian consumers trust homegrown brands for authenticity.

➢ **Variety and Experimentation:** Manufacturers constantly innovate with new flavors, designs, and features, giving businesses a wide range of options to choose from.

➢ **Eco-Friendly Options:** Sustainable products are on the rise, and private labels can easily adapt to this trend.

➢ **Online Sales:** E-commerce platforms are making it easier to reach customers and test new products.

In FMCG, private labeling offers a smart way to stay competitive. Anyone can experiment with new ideas without heavy investments, making it the ideal strategy to grow and scale quickly.

Why This Book?

This book isn't just about general ideas; it's about practical insights drawn from real experiences. Through these chapters, you'll understand how private labeling can help you grow your business 3x by building trust, minimizing expenses, and delivering quality products under your own brand.

The journey has just begun—let's explore how you can make private labeling your ultimate growth engine.

CHAPTER 2

Why Private Labeling?

Private labeling is a proven strategy for FMCG companies looking to scale their business with minimal risk and investment. By leveraging private label solutions, brand owners can reduce upfront investments, speed up market entry, and unlock new growth opportunities. Let's explore how private labeling provides **strategic advantages** and helps achieve **cost efficiency and speed to market.**

Strategic Advantages for FMCG Companies

➢ **Low Capex, Big Opportunities:** Private labeling allows companies to launch products without investing in expensive manufacturing facilities or supply chains. By outsourcing production to specialized manufacturers, businesses can save on infrastructure expenses while focusing on brand building and market expansion.

➢ **Custom Products, Stronger Brands:** With private labeling, you get complete control over your product's design, ingredients, and packaging. This customization helps create unique products that reflect your brand identity and connect better with your target audience.

> **Flexibility to Innovate:** Market trends in the FMCG sector can change overnight. Private labeling enables companies to experiment with new product ideas—whether it's flavors, packaging, or formulations—without the risk of high upfront costs. This flexibility empowers businesses to stay ahead of the curve.

> **Focus on Business Growth:** Instead of spending time and resources on managing production, private labeling allows FMCG companies to focus on marketing, distribution, and customer relationships. This leads to better efficiency and faster overall growth.

Cost Savings and Speed to Market

> **Minimal Investments, Maximum Returns:** Private labeling is ideal for businesses looking to enter the market with limited funds. It eliminates the need for heavy investments in equipment, raw materials, and workforce, making it a cost-effective solution for FMCG companies of all sizes.

> **Fast Product Launches:** Traditional product development can take months, if not years, due to complex manufacturing and supply chain setups. With private labeling, you can bring your product to market in a fraction of the time. Manufacturers already have established processes, ensuring quick turnarounds.

> **Reduced Overheads:** By partnering with private label manufacturers, you can avoid high operational expenses like inventory management and quality control. These savings can be redirected toward branding and customer acquisition, boosting your competitive edge.

> **Efficient Risk Management:** Launching a new product comes with uncertainties. Private labeling minimizes risks by sharing production and operational responsibilities with experienced manufacturers. This way, even small-scale businesses can explore new opportunities without fear of significant losses.

Case Studies: Success Stories and Transformative Impacts

1. Launching 15+ Products with Ease

When I first started working with Aditya Dalmia, I quickly realized that his approach to private labeling was unlike anything I had experienced before. Right after my first deal, I jokingly asked Aditya to match the rates of my regular production—something I thought was impossible. He simply smiled and explained that his solutions weren't designed for large-scale, high-quantity production but for short runs where flexibility and innovation matter most.

Over time, this philosophy proved invaluable. Aditya's team consistently delivered solutions that saved me time and effort. In fact, I've successfully launched over 15 new products with their support, each one with a seamless experience that felt less like outsourcing and more like working with an in-house team.

One of the standout benefits has been the speed and efficiency of our new product development (NPD). With Aditya's ready-to-deliver solutions and innovative strategies, we've been able to turn ideas into market-ready products faster than ever before.

Today, launching a new product is no longer a stressful or daunting process. Instead, it's a passion-driven journey made easy with a partner who understands my goals and delivers above expectations every time. Working with Aditya Dalmia has transformed the way we approach private labeling and product innovation.

2. From Uncertainty to Assurance: A Remarkable Journey

Running a business comes with its fair share of challenges, but our biggest hurdle was dealing with the constant uncertainties. Questions like, "Will there be cost transparency?" or "What happens if an error occurs?" kept troubling us. Quality issues were another concern—what if something went wrong? The anxiety only grew with thoughts like, "What if my competitor approaches them?" or "How will last-minute urgencies be handled?" The cherry on top of this uncertainty cake was, "How do I ensure 100% safety when I'm not present 24x7?"

Then we met **Mr. Aditya Goyal,** and let me just say—what a man he is! From the moment we started working with him, our perspective completely changed. Aditya didn't just answer our questions; he brought clarity to our chaos. He ensured that every concern was addressed in detail, leaving no room for doubt. His professionalism, coupled with his genuine commitment to his clients, made us feel secure in ways we had never experienced before.

With Aditya, it was like having an ally who understood our struggles and offered solutions tailored to us. Transparency in costs, quality assurance, and even handling emergencies—everything was taken care of without us having to stress. He built a partnership based on trust, so much so that the fear of competition or operational hiccups vanished completely.

Today, working with Aditya has become synonymous with peace of mind. He not only eliminated our uncertainties but gave us the confidence to expand and grow without worrying about the day-to-day challenges. If there's one word to describe our experience with Aditya, it's **transformational.**

Why Private Labeling is the Smart Choice?

Private labeling is not just a cost-cutting strategy; it's a smart way for FMCG businesses to innovate, grow, and thrive. By minimizing investments and leveraging the expertise of private label manufacturers, companies can focus on creating value for their customers.

In the next chapter, we'll discuss how to select the right private label partner and the key steps to ensure your products align with market expectations.

CHAPTER 3

Selecting the Right Private Label Partner

Choosing the right private label partner is one of the most crucial decisions for any FMCG business looking to succeed in the competitive market. The right partner can be the difference between a smooth product launch and one filled with unnecessary challenges. In this chapter, we'll explore the key criteria for selecting a private label partner and why **Vishnu Delight** stands out as a top choice for your FMCG needs.

1. **Criteria for Choosing a Partner: Experience, Capacity, and Innovation**

   When selecting a private label partner, there are several factors you must consider:

   - **Experience:** A partner with years of experience understands the market dynamics and knows how to handle the challenges of product development, quality control, and timely delivery. Look for a partner who has a proven track record of successfully launching products similar to what you have in mind.

- **Capacity:** Your partner must be able to meet your production demands without compromising on quality or timelines. Check whether they have the infrastructure and scalability to handle your current needs and future growth.

- **Innovation:** In a rapidly changing FMCG market, staying ahead of the competition requires constant innovation. Look for a partner who is proactive in exploring new trends and developing unique product offerings. This could include experimenting with flavors, packaging, or even introducing entirely new product categories.

- **Flexibility:** The market is dynamic, and businesses often face shifting consumer preferences, trends, and unforeseen challenges. A partner who is flexible can adapt quickly to these changes, ensuring your product line remains relevant and responsive.

2. **Evaluating Vishnu Delight's Legacy and Expertise**

When it comes to private labeling in the FMCG sector, Vishnu Delight offers an unmatched legacy and depth of expertise that can greatly benefit your business:

- **57 Years of Industry Legacy:** With over five decades of experience, Vishnu Delight has built a reputation as a trusted name in the FMCG sector. Their vast knowledge across diverse categories and consumer trends ensures unparalleled value for partners.

- **15,000+ Private-Label Products:** Vishnu Delight has successfully developed and launched over 15,000 private-label products, demonstrating their expertise in meeting diverse client needs and market demands.

- **Serving FMCG Giants:** Vishnu Delight proudly serves 3 out of 5 leading FMCG giants, showcasing their ability to deliver at scale and meet the highest industry standards.

- **Massive Production Capacity:** Operating across **8 state-of-the-art factories** and supported by a dedicated team of **1,700+ members**, the company produces **300+ tonnes of healthy snacks daily** for brands around the globe. With a total daily capacity of **550 tonnes** across snacks and biscuits, Vishnu Delight handles high-volume demands with ease.

- **Zero Investment & No MOQ Guaranteed:** Unlike many other private label partners, Vishnu Delight offers a zero-investment model with no minimum order quantity (MOQ). This ensures businesses can enter the market without heavy financial commitments, providing flexibility to scale at their own pace.

- **Nationwide Reach:** With operations in **4 states, 59 cities,** over **100 distributors,** and **5,000+ retail outlets,** Vishnu Delight ensures a robust supply chain and market presence.

- **Quality & Consistency:** True to their promise of **"Meri Factory Wala Trust"**, Vishnu Delight guarantees consistent product quality, packaging, and flavor in every production cycle. This focus on quality allows businesses to build a reliable private label without any compromises.

- **Cost Transparency & Genuine Pricing:** At Vishnu Delight, transparency is a cornerstone. All pricing details are shared upfront, with no hidden charges. Any price adjustments are logical, well-communicated, and justified, ensuring partners have complete clarity and trust.

- **Trust & Secrecy:** Vishnu Delight maintains strict confidentiality for all private label products. Whether it's proprietary recipes or packaging designs, the company ensures your intellectual property is safeguarded.

3. **Partnership Strategies: Building a Collaborative Framework**

A successful private label partnership is more than just a transaction. It is a collaboration that builds mutual trust and ensures both parties work toward a shared goal: successful product launches and long-term market presence. Here are some key strategies for creating a strong partnership framework:

- **Control at Every Stage:** A collaborative partnership allows you to maintain control over every aspect of your product, from the initial concept to the final packaging. With clear communication, you can ensure your vision and quality standards are met at each step of the process. This hands-on approach enables you to adapt quickly and make necessary changes along the way.

- **Transparency at Every Step:** A successful partnership is built on transparency. Regular updates, clear production timelines, and open communication ensure there are no surprises. This helps maintain smooth operations and allows you to make informed decisions, especially when changes or challenges arise.

- **Flexibility and Adaptability:** Flexibility in handling changes—whether it's tweaking the design, adjusting production volumes, or exploring new markets—is essential in a private label partnership. Working with a partner who is adaptable can help you stay competitive and meet customer demands without unnecessary delays.

- **Mutual Growth and Long-Term Vision:** Successful private label partnerships are those where both parties see the potential for growth and are committed to mutual success. The best partners look beyond short-term goals and focus on long-term strategies that benefit both businesses. This creates a strong foundation for sustained growth and profitability.

The Right Partner

Choosing the right partner is key to building a successful private label. It's not just about having the right experience and capacity, but about finding a partner who understands your goals, values your vision, and works with you to create something great.

By collaborating with a partner who offers control, transparency, and flexibility, you'll be in the driver's seat every step of the way. Whether it's quality, flavor, or delivery, you'll have the confidence that your private label product is in the best hands.

Remember, the right partnership is about mutual trust, growth, and a shared commitment to success.

CHAPTER 4

Comprehensive Guide to Outsourcing

Outsourcing is a strategic tool that can help your FMCG business grow without the heavy investments associated with setting up large-scale operations. Understanding when to outsource, what to outsource, and how to maintain control over quality and consistency is essential for achieving business success.

What to Outsource: Key Areas to Focus On

Outsourcing can free up valuable resources, especially for areas that require specialized knowledge or significant capital investment. The most common functions that are outsourced in the FMCG industry include:

➢ **Recipe and Product Development:** One of the most important things to understand about outsourcing is what functions are best left to external experts. Recipe development, for example, can be outsourced to specialists who have deep knowledge of food science, flavor combinations, and market trends. Outsourcing recipe development allows you to tap into innovative ideas that you may not have in-house and saves you the time and resources of developing them yourself.

➢ **Packaging and Design:** Packaging is not just about protecting your product; it's also a powerful marketing tool. Outsourcing packaging design helps you stay ahead of market trends, offering innovative designs that align with consumer expectations. Whether it's eco-friendly packaging or a unique design that enhances brand appeal, an external partner with packaging expertise can deliver high-quality results.

➢ **Manufacturing and Production:** Scaling up production often requires significant investment in machinery, labor, and infrastructure. By outsourcing manufacturing to trusted partners, you can access the right facilities and resources without the burden of capital expenditures. This model allows you to rapidly respond to demand changes, increase efficiency, and avoid over-investing in production capabilities that may not be required long-term.

Timing the Shift: Knowing When to Outsource and When to In-House

One of the key challenges in outsourcing is knowing the right time to outsource specific functions and when to bring them in-house. The decision of When to Outsource and When to go In-House should be driven by factors such as:

➢ **Capacity and Expertise:** When your internal resources lack the necessary expertise or your team is already stretched thin, outsourcing gives you immediate access to skills and technology. It's often the fastest way to grow and scale your operations.

➢ **Cost Efficiency:** Outsourcing helps to reduce overhead, especially when scaling production quickly without the need for upfront capital investments. This is particularly useful for new products or limited runs that don't justify the fixed expenses of in-house production.

➢ **When to Bring It In-House:** As your business becomes more established and your product lines become stable, bringing certain functions in-house, such as production, can offer better control and cost efficiency. Once you have the capacity and expertise, producing in-house can help you improve quality control and maintain product consistency.

Maintaining Quality and Consistency Through Outsourcing

Outsourcing brings financial advantages, but quality and consistency remain paramount. Strong vendor management ensures these standards are always met.

➢ **Clear Specifications:** One of the first steps in ensuring quality is providing clear, detailed product specifications to your outsourcing partner. From raw materials to packaging, defining every detail in advance ensures the final product meets your expectations.

➢ **Regular Quality Checks:** Just because you're outsourcing doesn't mean you should lose control over the quality of your product. Implement regular quality assurance checks and audits at different stages of the production process. This will help identify any discrepancies early on and avoid costly mistakes.

➢ **Open Communication:** Building a strong relationship with your outsourcing partner is essential. Keep the communication channels open and transparent to ensure that your partner understands your expectations and can raise any concerns before they become major issues.

The Power of Smart Outsourcing Decisions

Outsourcing is a game-changer for FMCG companies looking to grow rapidly without overcommitting capital. By carefully selecting which functions to outsource, strategically timing the shift, and maintaining strong quality control practices, you can drive efficiency, save money, and bring innovative products to market faster.

CHAPTER 5

Demystifying Private Labeling

Private labeling can be a powerful growth strategy for businesses in the FMCG sector, but many myths and misconceptions can make it seem more complicated than it is. This chapter will tackle the common misunderstandings, unveil the true realities of private labeling, and guide you on how to overcome the challenges, especially in terms of quality control and brand alignment.

1. **Addressing Common Myths and Misconceptions**

   Myth 1: Private Labeling Compromises Quality

   People often associate private labels with lower quality due to their competitive pricing. However, private label products are frequently manufactured using the same materials and processes as branded goods. The difference lies in branding, not quality.

   Myth 2: Private Labeling Requires Huge Investments

   Contrary to popular belief, private labeling isn't reserved for big players with deep pockets. Many manufacturers, like us, offer "zero investment" and "no MOQ" options, making it accessible even for small businesses.

Myth 3: Private Labeling Doesn't Build Brands

Some think private labeling undermines brand recognition. The truth is, it provides a unique opportunity to create a customized brand story, build loyalty, and stand out in the market through strategic design and marketing.

Myth 4: Private Labeling Limits Innovation

Many assume private labeling means sticking to generic products. In reality, it's an avenue to innovate, experiment with flavors, and introduce unique packaging that aligns with your brand's identity.

Myth 5: Private Labeling Offers No Long-Term Reliability

Another misconception is that private labeling partnerships are short-term or inconsistent. Reliable manufacturers prioritize transparency, quality, and a collaborative approach, ensuring long-lasting partnerships that grow alongside your brand.

2. Realities of the Private Labeling Industry

Private labeling is a strategic move that goes beyond cost-saving. It allows businesses to focus on branding and customer experience without worrying about manufacturing. The industry today emphasizes flexibility, innovation, and collaboration, making it a viable option for businesses of all sizes.

3. Overcoming Challenges: Quality Control and Brand Alignment

Quality Control: Our Approach

One of the most significant concerns clients have regarding private labeling is the assurance of product quality. The key to overcoming this challenge is a rigorous quality control process that ensures consistency at every stage of production.

In our factory, quality management is at the heart of everything we do. We have multiple checkpoints in place to ensure that the product meets the highest standards:

- **Raw Material Check:** We start by inspecting the raw materials to ensure they meet our quality criteria.

- **WIP (Work-in-Progress) Check:** During production, we monitor the progress to ensure that there are no deviations from the planned quality.

- **Finished Goods Check:** Once production is complete, the product is carefully inspected for any defects or discrepancies.

- **Packaging Check:** Finally, during the packaging process, a thorough quality check is conducted to ensure that the product is properly packed and ready for shipment.

Despite these thorough checks, if any quality issues arise, we take full responsibility. We replace the defective product and investigate the root cause to prevent similar issues from occurring in the future. Quality control is so important to us that even the smallest issue is treated like a serious problem that must be addressed immediately.

Brand Alignment: Maintaining Consistency

A key challenge in private labeling is ensuring that the product aligns with the brand's image. Our focus is on building strong, long-term relationships with our clients, ensuring that their vision is realized in every product we create. From packaging to flavor consistency, we work closely with brands to ensure the final product matches the desired image and standards.

Conclusion: Quality and Trust at the Core

Private labeling offers tremendous potential for growth, but success depends on overcoming challenges like quality control and brand alignment. By working with trusted partners, ensuring rigorous quality checks, and maintaining transparency throughout the process, businesses can confidently navigate the private labeling journey.

CHAPTER 6

The EASY Framework

Every day, we come across businesses that face countless challenges and feel uncertain about how to move forward. Maybe you've experienced some of these struggles yourself:

➢ **Trust Issues...** Is what's promised really going to be delivered?

➢ **Delivery Delays...** My order didn't arrive when it was supposed to!

➢ **Unclear Order Status...** I have no idea what's going on with my order!

➢ **Quality Variations...** The product quality keeps changing.

➢ **Mismatch with Samples...** The final product doesn't match the sample I was shown.

➢ **Small Orders, Big Problems...** When the order is small, the issues only get bigger!

➢ **Hidden Rules...** Replacement or return policies aren't clear until there's a problem!

➢ **Planning Struggles...** I can't plan my deliveries properly because everything feels uncertain.

➢ **Inconsistent Timings...** Sometimes things get done on time, sometimes they don't.

➢ **Cost Fluctuations...** The cost keeps changing all the time.

These are real struggles that many businesses face, and Vishnu Delight understands them. That's why we've created a solution—an **EASY Framework**—designed to take away the hassle, bring consistency, and ensure that your experience with us is smooth and stress-free.

We present to you the EASY Framework

E: Expertise

First and foremost, expertise is crucial. If you're looking for a partner who truly understands your needs and the intricacies of your business, you're in the right place.

➢ **Plant Operations:** You need plants that operate efficiently and consistently. We ensure that your manufacturing process is smooth and reliable.

➢ **Domain Knowledge:** Understanding market trends, customer demands, and competition is essential. Our expertise helps you make informed decisions at every stage.

➢ **Customization:** Building a unique brand identity is key. We assist in tailoring your products to perfectly align with your vision.

➢ **Adaptability:** Every business is different, and we work with you to adapt your brand in a way that resonates perfectly with your customers.

A: Authenticity

To make your private label successful, authenticity is the foundation. Keeping your product line genuine and true to its promise is essential.

> **Flavors & Formulation:** We ensure that the flavors and formulations of your products are authentic and true to your standards.

> **Trade Practices:** Transparency is vital to us, but secrecy is equally important in protecting your intellectual property.

> **Ethics & Transparency:** We conduct our business with honesty and integrity, ensuring everything is clear and transparent.

> **Overall Quality:** We guarantee the quality of every product, so your customers are never disappointed.

S: Strength

The true strength of your business lies in your team and operations. Strength here means building strong, scalable operations.

> **Team Skills:** Our team is skilled in driving innovation and efficiency, helping your business adapt to new challenges.

> **Operational Efficiency:** Streamlining operations means maximizing resources and reducing waste, making your business more effective.

> **Innovation:** We're constantly working on new ideas and solutions, ensuring that your business remains ahead in the market.

> **Scaling Up:** As your business grows, a strong foundation is critical. We're here to help you build that foundation to scale effectively.

Y: Yes Deal

Lastly, Y stands for embracing every opportunity with a "Yes." Change is inevitable, and exploring new solutions is vital to success.

> **Embrace Change:** We help you stay agile and adapt as the market evolves. Flexibility is key to growth.

> **Listen & Show:** It's not just about hearing feedback — it's about taking action and showing you value it.

> **Discuss & Detail:** Open communication with partners is crucial. Every detail matters in building a strong partnership.

> **Reality Check:** Regularly evaluate your journey to ensure you stay on track toward your goals.

> **"Meri Factory Wali Feel":** It's essential to choose a factory partner who makes you feel like you're part of their family, with transparent communication and mutual respect.

Your Business GPS – No More U-turns!

The EASY Framework is a roadmap that will guide you in scaling your business effectively. It provides the support you need at every stage, ensuring you can navigate your private label journey with confidence and efficiency. Make every decision with care, and implement the right strategies to successfully establish your brand in the market.

The Future of Private Labeling in the Food Industry

The food industry is constantly evolving. What worked yesterday might not work today, and the same goes for private labeling. As consumer preferences change and technology advances, private label food brands need to stay ahead of the game to continue growing.

Innovations and Technologies Shaping the Future

Here's how innovation is transforming the private label food business:

➢ **Smart Manufacturing:** Technology is helping manufacturers produce food more efficiently. With smart machines and real-time tracking, brands can reduce waste and improve quality. This means quicker production, fewer mistakes, and better products for consumers.

➢ **Sustainability:** Consumers care more than ever about the environment. Using eco-friendly packaging and sourcing ingredients responsibly are key trends. Brands that embrace sustainability will not only attract more customers but also improve overall efficiency and enhance profitability.

➢ **Automation and AI:** In the future, automation will be a game-changer. AI can predict consumer demand, helping businesses make smarter decisions about production. This helps avoid overstocking or running out of popular items, leading to better inventory management and enhanced financial performance.

➢ **Better Transparency:** With growing concerns over food safety and quality, consumers want to know where their food comes from. Blockchain and other technologies are making it easier for brands to show the journey of their products— from farm to table—building trust and credibility.

Predicting Market Movements and Consumer Trends

Understanding what's coming next in the market is crucial. Here are some trends you should watch out for:

➢ **Health Consciousness:** People are more focused on their health, and that's showing in their food choices. Private label brands that offer healthier options—like low-sugar snacks, gluten-free biscuits, or high-protein nuts—will likely see a surge in demand.

➢ **Convenience:** Busy lifestyles are making convenience foods more popular. Products like ready-to-eat snacks, portion-controlled packs, and easy-to-open packages are becoming staples for many consumers. Brands that provide convenience without compromising on quality will stand out.

> **Personalization:** Customers want products that fit their specific needs. Whether it's a snack that meets dietary restrictions or a biscuit with a unique flavor, personalization is key. Brands that offer customizable products or cater to niche diets will have an edge in the market.

> **Online Shopping:** More people are buying food online than ever before. Private label brands that invest in strong online marketing and make their products easily available through e-commerce platforms will capture a larger share of the market.

> **Plant-Based & Natural Ingredients:** Consumers are moving towards more plant-based and natural food options. Whether it's plant-based snacks or biscuits with minimal artificial ingredients, offering cleaner, healthier products is a trend that's only going to grow.

Preparing Your Brand for the Future

The future of private labeling in the food industry is bright. As technology advances and consumer preferences shift towards health-conscious, sustainable, and convenient products, private label brands have plenty of opportunities to grow. By staying on top of these trends and adapting to changes, your brand can not only survive but thrive in the competitive food market.

Focus on what your customers want, be open to new innovations, and always aim for quality.

⊘ ⊘ ⊘ ⊘

CHAPTER 8

Vishnu Delight's Impact on FMCG Growth

At Vishnu Delight, we're more than just a partner in your private labeling journey; we're the catalyst that accelerates your FMCG brand's growth. The secret to our success lies in our deep understanding of the food industry, innovation, and a commitment to delivering consistent, high-quality products. Our focus is not just to meet expectations, but to exceed them. This unique approach has helped our clients achieve 3x growth, paving the way for them to dominate the market.

How Vishnu Delight Helps Clients Achieve 3x Growth

1. **Expertise in the Food Industry:** Our team's rich experience in the FMCG sector ensures that we understand the challenges and opportunities your brand faces. We know that success in private labeling isn't just about offering quality products – it's about anticipating market trends, consumer behavior, and adapting swiftly. By leveraging our expertise, clients can streamline their operations, make informed decisions, and position their products for maximum impact.

2. **Innovation in Product Development:** At Vishnu Delight, we prioritize innovation. Whether it's introducing healthier options, catering to specific dietary preferences, or creating convenient packaging, we are always ahead of the curve. Our clients benefit from this innovation, allowing them to offer fresh and relevant products that resonate with today's consumers. This proactive approach to product development directly contributes to growth, ensuring our clients never fall behind in an ever-evolving market.

3. **Consistency and Quality Assurance:** Trust is crucial in FMCG. With Vishnu Delight, our clients can rely on consistent product quality, delivery on time, and seamless operations. This consistency builds customer loyalty, which in turn fuels brand growth. By eliminating the common pain points like delivery delays, quality variations, and unexpected costs, we enable our clients to focus on scaling their business while we handle the logistics and production smoothly.

4. **Scalable Solutions for Growth:** As your business grows, your challenges change. At Vishnu Delight, we understand that scaling requires more than just increased production – it requires systems, strategies, and support that grow with you. We provide scalable solutions, from expanding your product range to optimizing your supply chain. Our clients benefit from flexible solutions that can adapt as their brand gains momentum in the market.

5. **Customer-Centric Approach:** Ultimately, the key to 3x growth is understanding and catering to customer needs. By

focusing on delivering what customers want — be it healthy snacks, indulgent treats, or convenient on-the-go options — our clients have managed to stay relevant and build a strong, loyal customer base. We help our clients keep a pulse on consumer preferences and market trends, ensuring their brand always stays one step ahead.

Success Stories: Clients Who Have Scaled Rapidly with EASY Framework

1. **The EASY Formula for Success:** When we partnered with **Vishnu Delight,** one big concern was: "How will I ensure 100% safety as I'm not there 24x7?" That's when they introduced us to the **EASY Framework,** and it truly lived up to its name—simple yet revolutionary.

   They assured us with their "meri factory wala trust," taking over the manufacturing hassles and letting us dedicate our time to marketing and growth. The EASY Framework turned out to be a game-changer, streamlining every step, eliminating uncertainties, and delivering consistent excellence. With their promise, "Aapka product chalega, toh humara kaam chalega," we knew we were in safe hands.

2. **EASY Solutions for Last-Minute Orders!:** Last-minute urgencies used to be a major challenge for us, but with the EASY Framework, everything changed. At Vishnu Delight, we always start by understanding our client's seasonality, order frequency, and quantities. This allows us to anticipate potential urgencies and plan accordingly.

However, when urgency strikes, we don't panic. Instead, we analyze the situation thoroughly and take immediate action, ensuring that your order is delivered as per your needs. Thanks to the EASY Framework, we've managed to successfully handle 75 out of 100 urgent cases with ease, allowing our clients to rest assured even in high-pressure situations.

With EASY, we make sure last-minute urgencies aren't a roadblock but an opportunity for us to show our commitment and efficiency.

CHAPTER 9

Building a Winning Strategy with Private Labeling

Building a private label brand is an exciting journey, but it requires a clear strategy to succeed. Whether you're starting from scratch or aiming to scale, it's essential to follow a systematic approach that ensures growth while maintaining the integrity of your brand and keeping customers loyal.

From Start-up to Scale: Navigating the Growth Ladder

1. **Start with the Right Product:** The foundation of your brand is the product itself. Focus on identifying a gap in the market or a need that's not being fully met. Your product should stand out with superior quality or unique features. Once you've nailed that, build your brand around it with clear messaging and a strong identity.

2. **Prioritize Consistency:** As your business grows, consistency becomes crucial. Your customers must know what to expect each time they purchase from you. Whether it's flavor,

texture, packaging, or overall experience, consistency helps build trust and keeps customers coming back.

3. **Scale Smartly:** Scaling too fast can lead to problems, but scaling strategically can help you expand your brand steadily. Increase your product range, optimize your supply chain, and gradually enter new markets. Focus on building a strong base before diving into rapid growth.

4. **Leverage Technology for Efficiency:** As your business expands, consider using technology to streamline operations. From inventory management to marketing automation, the right tools can help you scale faster without sacrificing quality.

Maintaining Brand Integrity and Customer Loyalty

1. **Stay True to Your Values:** As you grow, never lose sight of your brand's core values. Whether it's delivering quality or offering ethical sourcing, customers choose brands they trust. Keep delivering on your promises and remain transparent about your business practices.

2. **Keep the Customer at the Center:** Your customers should always be the focus. Listen to their feedback, whether it's positive or negative, and use it to improve your products and services. Personalize your offerings and ensure your customer service is top-notch to create loyal fans of your brand.

3. **Be Adaptable:** The market changes quickly, and so do customer preferences. Stay flexible and adapt to new trends or demands. Whether it's offering healthier alternatives or sustainable packaging, being able to evolve will keep your brand relevant in the long run.

Scale Up, Label Right!

Building a winning strategy for private labeling requires careful planning, attention to detail, and a focus on growth at the right pace. By maintaining brand integrity and keeping customers at the heart of your business, you can scale successfully and build a lasting, loyal customer base.

Conclusion

Throughout this journey, we've seen how Vishnu Delight empowers your brand with essential tools for growth. The GRID system, a core strength, helps streamline processes, making TIME SAVING and MONEY SAVING a priority. With this, you gain the FREEDOM TO EXPAND without any stress about the operational challenges. You maintain 100% CONTROL over your brand's direction, ensuring that every product aligns with your vision. The "Meri Wali Feeling" represents our commitment to making you feel like part of the family, delivering an output that reflects your values and resonates with your customers.

At Vishnu Delight, we believe the foundation of a successful brand lies in collaboration and innovation. As we look ahead, the private labeling space is brimming with exciting opportunities.

We encourage future collaborations that are driven by creativity and mutual growth. By staying ahead of trends, embracing cutting-edge technologies, and fostering open partnerships, we can collectively shape the future of private labeling. Together, we can unlock new possibilities, innovate boldly, and build lasting success in our industry.

So, let's keep the innovation rolling and the snacks crisp. After all, we're all in this to make your brand the next big thing!

Stress or Success – Your Call!

Now you're at a crossroads, with two paths ahead. The decision is yours to make, and whatever choice you make, we hope it takes your brand to new heights!

Keep working in an environment where "savdhani hati durgahtna gati" – 24x7 surveillance, constant follow-ups, and the stress of non-stop management. Is that really the path you want?

OR

Have us by your side and operate your "meri wali factory" – zero investment, zero MOQ, and 100% peace of mind. Let us handle the hard work while you focus on stress-free growth.

If you're leaning toward the second option, it's simple! Just connect with us, and we'll get things rolling. You can easily schedule a one-on-one meeting with us:

Your Email:

The choice is yours. Let's build something amazing together!